Original title:
Lilac Lines

Copyright © 2025 Creative Arts Management OÜ
All rights reserved.

Author: Riley Donovan
ISBN HARDBACK: 978-1-80566-652-3
ISBN PAPERBACK: 978-1-80566-937-1

Imprints of Lavish Gardens

In gardens bright, where chaos reigns,
The gnomes play pranks and forget their names.
A bee with sass steals all the blooms,
While squirrels plot, in shady rooms.

A flower says, 'Hey, that's my spot!'
As petals scatter, laughter's caught.
The daisies dance in a silly trance,
While tulips giggle in the sun's romance.

A Palette Paints the Air

Spray cans clash in colors bold,
As nature laughs at rules of old.
A rainbow's spill, like candy's grace,
Makes puddles blush, a dizzying place.

The daisies dream of karaoke nights,
Singing tunes that shine so bright.
With every stroke, the joke's not shy,
As paintbrushes paint the butterflies.

Murmurs of the Serene Shade

In the shade where shadows jest,
Chickens gossip, they love a fest.
The oak tree chuckles, branches sway,
As lizards plot their great getaway.

Leaves whisper secrets of the day,
In a symphony of breezy play.
While squirrels hold their nutty meetings,
With acorns flying, laughter's greetings.

Enigma in the Garden's Glow

Beneath the moon, the flowers scheme,
As night unveils its wacky dream.
A pumpkin grins, a squash looks sly,
They swap their hats and giggle high.

The fireflies dance, a twinkling show,
While nightingale jokes steal the glow.
With every flicker, mischief's spun,
In this garden, laughs have won.

The Language of Mauve Mornings

The sun yawns wide, it's time to rise,
With toast and jam, a feast of sighs.
Birds gossip loud, they spill their tea,
While squirrels dance, so wild and free.

Neighbors peek through their window blinds,
In slippers and robes, unique designs.
A dance-off starts, unplanned and bright,
With laughter ringing like pure delight.

A Symphony of Grape-Scented Air

Balloons float high, a silly balloon,
While kids chase giggles under the moon.
Jelly beans tumble, candy galore,
As laughter fills the air, we want more.

A cat in a hat grins from a tree,
Telling bad puns, oh, woe is he!
His jokes are odd, but hearts they win,
In grape-scented air, let the fun begin!

Cascading Tones of Blooming Tales

Flowers gossip, they whisper and sway,
Telling tales of the crazy day.
Bees join in, buzzing their rhyme,
While butterflies dance, oh, so sublime.

A snail in a shell, slow as can be,
Winks at a frog with a cup of tea.
Where blooms giggle and scents collide,
The world is a stage, let laughter abide!

Petal Paths of Enchanted Evenings

The moon wears shades, a funky old friend,
As night takes hold, and fun won't end.
Stars flicker like lights in a bistro,
While shadows sway, throwing quite a show.

Crickets sing tunes, flat and off-key,
Yet we bob our heads; it's all quite free.
In paths of petals, where joy weaves tight,
We dance to the rhythm of silly delight.

Beckoning Darkness

In the shadows, squirrels dance,
With nuts that roll and oft' mischance.
A cat stuck high in a tree,
Meows for help, a sight to see.

Beneath the moon, a raccoon grins,
Stealing snacks like it's his sins.
The night is filled with quirky sounds,
As laughter echoes all around.

Gentle Light

Morning brings a goofy glow,
The sun decides to steal the show.
A rooster crows, but sounds like glee,
Frogs hop along, full of esprit.

Butterflies wear silly hats,
Chasing bees and dancing cats.
With all the giggles in the air,
It's hard to tell just who's the bear!

Ode to the Secret Garden

In hidden spots, the gnomes all laugh,
Their tea parties are just a gaffe.
With cups that spill like laughter loud,
They curtsy low, to joy, they're bowed.

Flowers wear their finest shoes,
While bees play tag with squirrels' snooze.
Beneath the leaves, the rabbit hops,
With floppy ears, it never stops.

A Dance in a Violet Dreamscape

In purple realms where dreams take flight,
A worm does tango, quite a sight!
While daisies clap and poppies cheer,
The grasshoppers join in the jeer.

The sky gets tickled by stray clouds,
As all the creatures waltz in crowds.
With giggles that spill from petals bright,
They dance till dawn, a pure delight.

Harmonizing with the Petal Flow

Petals swirl in tune so sweet,
As ants march by with tiny feet.
They sing a song of summer's cheer,
A bumblebee buzzes, "Hey, come here!"

With kites that soar on gentle breeze,
The world seems light, our hearts at ease.
In every shade, a joke's unveiled,
Nature's laughter, never failed.

Whispers in Lavender

In a field where odd socks roam,
There's a gnome who dreams of foam.
He dances with the bees so bold,
Telling tales of socks turned gold.

Each flower laughs as he stumbles,
While the wind giggles and tumbles.
A cat in shades of purple prance,
Invites him in for a frolicsome dance.

Lemonade drips from honeyed vines,
As squirrels debate the best wine.
While daisies gossip without a care,
About the gnome's bright purple hair.

And when the sun begins to fade,
They play charades in the glade.
With whispers soft and giggles loud,
They paint their world with laughter proud.

Petals of Dawn

A chicken wearing a sunhat bright,
Struts around from morn till night.
With each step, she honks a tune,
Beneath a sleepy, yawning moon.

The daisies giggle and twirl about,
While mushrooms murmur with a pout.
'The rooster should really take a nap,'
They cluck around in a friendly flap.

A snail slides by with a flair so keen,
Wearing shades in the early sheen.
He grins at the chicken, strikes a pose,
While petals fall like giggling toes.

And with the dawn, their antics spree,
As they sip on dew with glee.
In a carnival of bloom and cheer,
Petals of dawn bring laughter near.

Echoes of Springtime Dreams

A frog in a bow tie croaks so fine,
His best friend, a lizard, sips on wine.
They throw a bash on a lily pad,
Inviting critters, both good and bad.

The butterflies flutter with flair and grace,
While crickets keep time in a jazzy space.
With a wink, the lizard takes the stage,
As the frog creates waves of ribbeting rage.

A bunny joins in, just for the fun,
With a top hat and a sparkly bun.
They dance 'round the reeds with a theatrical scream,
In the echoes of all their springtime dreams.

As marshmallow clouds drift above their groove,
They twirl 'til the stars feel the need to move.
In a nighttime jamboree filled with delight,
The world's a circus come nightfall bright.

Shades of Purple Twilight

A turtle with tales of the sea,
Wears a cloak of lavender, just to be free.
He claims to ride waves on a flamingo flight,
But truth be told, he just loves the night.

The owls hoot while the bunnies hop,
As colors melt into a candy-top.
They gather round for a riddle game,
With giggles that echo, never the same.

A squirrel with charm and a wink so sly,
Stages a play with a big, silly pie.
As they gather 'round, their laughter swells,
With crumbs and cookies and funny tales to tell.

At twilight's peak, friendships ignite,
In shades of purple, everything feels right.
With every chuckle that fills the air,
They weave their dreams without a care.

Shadows of Lavender Dreams

In a garden of giggles, the colors collide,
Fluffy bunnies skip, while caterpillars hide.
With whispers of laughter, the flowers all sway,
Chasing the butterflies, they frolic and play.

The bees wear tiny hats, buzzing with glee,
As they trade secret recipes for sweet honey tea.
Rabbits argue loudly, who's faster in flight,
While squirrels in tuxedos dance under the light.

The sun starts to chuckle, as shadows grow long,
Twirling in sync with their favorite song.
Each petal tells stories, of mishaps and cheer,
Sprinkling joy on the shrubs, whispering near.

When day gives a wink, and twilight comes round,
Frogs start a band, with a ribbiting sound.
Laughter lingers softly, on the warm breeze's sway,
In a world made of colors, where silliness plays.

The Dance of Plum Petals

In the orchard, where pranks bloom and thrive,
The plums tease the apples, trying to jive.
They roll down the branches, giggling in tow,
While cherries on top join the dance, oh so slow.

The wind, like a DJ, spins tunes from the trees,
As lemons join in, with a twist and a tease.
With every sweet shuffle, a nutty surprise,
Watch out for the peaches, those crafty spies!

A raccoon in shades, sets the scene quite bright,
Pops out with a wink, causing some fright.
With slinky grape vines, they wiggle anew,
Swaying like dancers, each fruit in full view.

When the sun starts to bow, and stars take a bow,
The laughter continues, with a gleeful "wow!"
In the rhythm of ripeness, they sing all night long,
Celebrating their harvest, with a jubilant song.

Echoes of Amethyst Twilight

As the twilight descends, magic begins,
Fairies in giggles, with mischievous grins.
Their wands made of sparkles, they twirl in delight,
Playing hide-and-seek with shadows of night.

The moon starts a joke, about the stars' bright game,
While owls with monocles join in with no shame.
With a flap of their wings, they share silly plots,
Trading stories of squirrels who wear goofy hats.

The lavender whispers, "Dare we take flight?"
With a flop and a tangle, they glow in moonlight.
Bouncing on clouds, like marshmallows float,
They create a ruckus, aboard a nightboat.

When dawn peeks with laughter, and colors entwine,
Tales of their pranks blend with morning's design.
So, if you hear chuckles beneath the sky's hue,
It's the echoes of twilight, just waiting for you.

Serenade of Faded Blooms

In a patch where the faded blooms settle with sass,
A sunflower chuckles, "Will you join me, alas?"
With daisies all giggling at the tales they'll weave,
They share syrupy secrets, you wouldn't believe.

A dandelion yells, "Let's blow dreams on the breeze!"
As petals all flutter, with a graceful tease.
An old rose sighs deeply, "Time's not on our side,
But laughter is timeless, let's spread it with pride."

The clovers conspire, wearing hats made of dew,
While bugs on guitars strum a funny tune.
They sway with the rhythm, their colors aflush,
As a dragonfly leads them, in a whimsical rush.

When twilight approaches, and the world starts to rest,
The faded blooms whisper, "We've had quite a jest."
With memories of giggles, in the soft afterglow,
They know that tomorrow will bring more to show.

Twilight's Tender Embrace

In the garden, blooms collide,
Colors clash, oh what a ride!
Petals tumble, they slip and slide,
Laughing flowers, bursting with pride.

Dancing shadows, waltzing around,
Whispers floating, a silly sound.
Bees in tuxedos, what a sight!
Buzzing jokes till the morning light.

Garden gnomes join in the fray,
Telling secrets, come what may.
They trip on roots, full of grace,
With silly smiles upon their face.

The moon winks, sending a clue,
Nature's jesters are feeling blue.
When twilight falls, the laughter grows,
In this bloom dance, anything goes!

The Fading Echo of Scented Hues

Petals giggle, colors play,
Underneath the sun's soft ray.
Every fragrance tells a tale,
Of bumblebees on a merry trail.

Noses twitch, scents do swirl,
Dandelions in a twirl.
The daisies whisper, 'What a prank!'
While violets sit, drew a blank.

A breeze sneezes, flowers sway,
"Cut it out!" the roses say.
Lavenders chuckle, what a scene,
In this fragrant world, they reign supreme.

As shadows stretch, the jokes expand,
Each bloom knows humor's grand plan.
With each petal, a smile is grown,
In this colorful riot, joy is sown!

Mosaic of Petal Whispers

A mosaic spills across the floor,
With whispers soft, they beg for more.
Pansies giggle, holding court,
Joking 'bout a flower sport.

The daisies think they're such a catch,
While tulips scheme a clever hatch.
Petals flutter, trying to cheer,
On the breeze, jokes disappear.

Colors blend, like a wild dance,
Every bloom takes a chance.
Shrubs laugh loud, branches sway,
"Petal power on display!"

A basket full of hues and jokes,
Each bloom's laughter gently pokes.
This floral party never ends,
In petals' chatter, joy descends!

Colors of an Unwritten Story

Colors splash, a tale unfolds,
In the garden's gentle hold.
A daffodil tells a joke anew,
While petunias take a bow, too.

Buds shake hands, with roots so deep,
In petals' laughter, secrets keep.
A story danced in fragrant hue,
Twirled with sunlight, fresh as dew.

Each bloom shares tales of bliss,
With a wink, not one is amiss.
Willow trees roll their eyes and sigh,
At the silly things that flowers try.

A bud's bright giggle lights the day,
As flower friends laugh in disarray.
This haute garden comedy glows,
In every color, hilarity flows!

Violet Vows Under Starry Canopies

Under a sky with twinkling jokes,
We make promises to silly folks.
With twirls and spins, we dance in glee,
Wearing hats that are far too free.

The moon gives winks with its bright smirk,
As fireflies laugh, they play and lurk.
In a symphony of giggles, we vow,
To never pass on cake—even now!

Fragrant Chords of the Dusk

At twilight's gate where scents collide,
We strum a tune, the crickets guide.
Breezes chuckle in playful curls,
As petals blush and sway with swirls.

With laughter bursting in fragrant trails,
We sail on dreams with whimsy sails.
A symphony of oddities bloom,
Each note a giggle in the gloom.

Hues of Twilight Reverie

In violet shades, our thoughts unfold,
With tales of silliness, brave and bold.
Clouds drift by with a chuckling tune,
While we share secrets with the moon.

Laughter echoes through painted skies,
As winks and nudges come in surprise.
Dreams swirl like colors in the night,
Creating moments of sheer delight.

Garden of Wistful Dreams

In a garden where the laughter grows,
We dance with gnomes who strike funny poses.
Sunshine giggles as we run and play,
Chasing shadows that wiggle away.

Whimsical flowers bloom with a grin,
Tickling our hearts as we spin and spin.
In this space of gentle glee,
Even the trees join in, you see!

Tapestry of Fragrance

In a garden of scents, quite a mess,
Tiny bees dance, what a funny dress!
Petals flapping like they've found a tune,
Singing loudly 'We're all getting prunes!'

A squirrel strolls in, with a cheeky grin,
Pawing through blossoms, he'll surely win.
He lifts a single flower, holding it high,
"Look at me, I'm a tree, oh my, oh my!"

A butterfly whispers secrets so sweet,
"Let's take a break, you have two left feet!"
But off they go, painting the air,
Such silliness floats, without a care!

The sun chuckles down, warming each petal,
Nature giggles; there's no need to settle.
With laughter and color, the day is a spree,
In this fragrant tapestry, all are carefree!

Echoes of a Past Spring

Remember the tulips wearing leaf hats?
Mazily swaggering among old cats?
Echoes of laughter from when we were small,
Now they're just whispers, we still have a ball.

A dandelion pranks with its fluffy head,
Blowing the wish that we all should spread.
"Pick me, pick me!" the blossoms all shout,
But only the weeds seem to dance about.

Suddenly a robin steals a sweet twirl,
A worm dangles down, giving a whirl.
What is this chaos? Why does it spin?
Nature's soft flop, takes us right in.

With colors still vivid, spring is alive,
Such hilarious antics make worries dive.
Each bloom has a laugh, each tree has a grin,
Echoes of joy as funny tales begin!

Hidden Stories Underneath the Bloom

Underneath the bloom, secrets do hide,
A ladybug beams with a wink and a slide.
"Did you see the frog? Such a silly glide!"
In the jolly garden, laughter's our guide.

With roots intertwined like stories spun tight,
The flowers are whispering all through the night.
"Remember that bee, in his buzzing ballet?
He tripped on a petal and fumbled away!"

The ants hold a meeting, marching in cheer,
Discussing the food, yet still sharing beer.
"Hey, pass me that crumb, they said it was grand!"
As they nibble and giggle, they form a band.

Each petal, a chapter, each stem, a tall tale,
With mischief and humor, none will ever pale.
These hidden stories will always resound,
Underbulbs laughing, joy is unbound!

A Symphony of Color and Scent

Amidst the blooms, a symphony plays,
With petals like notes dancing in rays.
A rose starts a waltz, while the daisies hum,
While violets chuckle, all together, they strum.

The zinnias shout with colors so bright,
"Join us, join us, in this joyful delight!"
A daffodil trumpets, a chic little sound,
While lilies sway softly, round and around.

But wait, there's a cactus, feeling quite shy,
"Not too close, folks! I might prick if you try!"
The crowd erupts in a giggly surprise,
As humor and colors tango and rise.

Nature's own band plays songs in the air,
With laughter and scents that are wonderfully rare.
In this vibrant garden, tunes dance in spree,
A symphony of life, forever carefree!

The Color of Nostalgic Days

In a garden with hues so bright,
Wore my socks different, what a sight!
A neighbor chuckled, they couldn't believe,
Colorful chaos, I just had to weave.

Petals swirling in the sun's warm laugh,
A butterfly danced, it lost its path.
I stumbled too, but hey, what the fuss?
The weeds and I shared a mutual trust.

Memories bloom like daisies in spring,
When grass stains and giggles do their thing.
A kite got tangled in the old oak tree,
Just like my lunch, stuck inside me!

With colors that whisper, tales they unfold,
Of ice cream drips and candies bold.
I'll paint a smile with every hue,
As long as they don't name it blue!

Timeless Whispers Among the Stems

Whispers of bees buzz sweet little tunes,
As I search for my lost spoons under the moons.
They giggle and dart, avoiding my gaze,
Just like my dog when I call him for days!

In the midst of green, secrets entwine,
I mislaid my hat, now it's a shrine.
Blossoms giggle, oh what a show,
While I try to dance, look at me go!

Time winks at us from the old willow tree,
Every breeze carrying laughter for free.
I tripped over roots, oh what a surprise,
Even flowers giggled, with bulging eyes!

Yet roses refuse to share their perfume,
Claiming it's mine, but who needs this gloom?
Let's toast to friendships, old and new,
With daisies and jokes, as silly as glue!

A Reverie of Blooming Solitude

In quiet corners where flowers retreat,
I pondered life, and then lost my seat.
The daisies laughed as they witnessed my fall,
While shadows whispered, urging me to crawl.

Each bloom a secret, a silly jest,
As I wore my garden like a fuzzy vest.
Petals tickled my nose, oh what a tease,
A sneeze echoed wildly, rustling the leaves!

In solitude's grip, I danced like a fool,
Spinning with poppies, they made me drool.
A waltz with the weeds, an elegant mess,
Who knew flowers could bring such distress?

Yet laughter erupted, with colors aglow,
As birds chirped stories, putting on quite a show.
In the heart of the field, where mischief aligns,
I found all my joys in the craziest signs!

Secrets Beneath the Petals

In the garden where blooms conspire,
Buzzing bees all dressed in attire.
They gossip 'neath petals, oh what a tease,
Sharing secrets in a light summer breeze.

A riddle in roots, what do they hide?
A snack for the ants or a wild bug ride?
All the flowers whisper, 'Can you keep still?'
While the garden giggles, bending to thrill.

Their colors burst forth with a riotous flair,
But the daisies grumble, 'We don't want to share!'
Beneath twirling leaves, a laugh or a sigh,
As the tulips grinch, "Oh my, oh my!"

So come take a peek at their floral jest,
In the realm of the petals, they're truly the best!
A world all aglow, with stories galore,
Where laughter blooms bright, and they always want more!

Dance of the Swaying Stems

The stems do a dance, it's quite a sight,
Twisting and turning in soft morning light.
The daisies prance, with a bob and a weave,
While the roses just sigh, 'We'll never believe!'

With a flap and a flop, they sync to the beat,
Jumping and jiving, they can't find their feet.
The lilies just chuckle, shaking their heads,
As the sunflowers sway, all decked out in threads.

A breeze joins the party, a whimsical ghost,
Twirling the petals and making them boast.
"Look at us spin, we're so light on our toes!"
Said the poppies, with giggles that nobody knows.

The garden's alive with a marvelous flair,
Who knew swaying stems could dance in mid-air?
So join in the fun, let your worries unfurl,
And sway with the flowers, it's a whimsical world!

The Heart of a Garden in Bloom

In the center of colors, chaos unfurls,
The heart of the garden, where laughter twirls.
Bees buzzing funny, with jokes up their sleeves,
They tickle the petals, and spin like leaves.

The roses compete, with a wink and a grin,
'Who's the fairest?' they ask, a determined spin.
But the violets chuckle, 'We're small but we shine!'
As they giggle and sway, full of joyful vine.

The daisies all tumble, they trip and fall down,
But get back up laughing, without a frown.
As the daffodils hum, a silly old tune,
While clouds roll on by in a late afternoon.

With all this commotion, it's hard to ignore,
The heart of the garden, blooms wide and more.
So come take a look, at this jubilant scene,
Where laughter erupts in colors so keen!

Dreams Spun in Violet

In a lavender dream, where the giggles flow,
The petals come alive, putting on a show.
They wrap up their dreams, in a purple delight,
With whispers of joy, under stars so bright.

The midnight blooms chuckle, in their lovely attire,
Playing hide and seek, as shadows conspire.
With the moon as their witness, they dance 'round the bliss,
In a world made of laughter, you can't help but miss!

The bees join the fun, with a buzz and a hype,
Creating sweet chaos, it's a garden-type gripe.
"Oh dear!" said the tulips, "What's all this ruckus?"
But they can't help but laugh, feeling glad they just fuss.

So dreams spun in violet, floating like a kite,
Remind us of whimsy that dances at night.
In the garden of giggles, where silliness reigns,
Join the floral fiesta, where laughter remains!

Fluid Poetry of Petals

In a garden absurd, where petals float,
The bees wear boots, and butterflies gloat.
They dance in a circle, on the grass they twirl,
Chasing after napkins, in spring's grand whirl.

A squirrel in shades, sipping tea all day,
Shares secrets with flowers, in a comical way.
They plot a parade, with giggles and cheer,
While flower pots tremble, their humor sincere.

When raindrops arrive, they hold a road show,
Like umbrellas in shoes, they waddle to and fro.
Onward they march, in floral disguise,
Amidst laughter and pollen, their joy never dies.

With each twist and turn, they tickle the air,
A chorus of chuckles, under sunshine's glare.
The petals all whisper, in colors so bright,
Fluid poetry blooms, bringing endless delight.

Shadows in the Orchard's Embrace

In the orchard, shadows play a grand game,
The apples are giggling, they're never the same.
With whispers of mischief, they dangle and sway,
While squirrels tell stories, and save the day.

The pears wear glasses, quite wise and absurd,
They discuss the latest on flying birds.
Underneath the branches, in whimsical cheer,
Even the wind stops, just to lend an ear.

Chasing the shadows, the chickens parade,
In boot-scootin' dances, their clucking displayed.
The carrots giggle, as they hide in the dirt,
While the broccoli laughs, in its leafy green shirt.

It's a merry affair, in twilight's caress,
With shadows performing, they aim to impress.
In the orchard's embrace, where laughter prevails,
The fruits tell their tales, in amusing details.

Whispers of Purple Hues

In a world of giggles, the flowers convene,
With whispers of purple, oh what a scene!
Daisies play poker, the roses sing low,
While violets tell jokes, that steal the show.

A butterfly busts a move with great flair,
The zinnias chuckle, then twirl in the air.
They toss around petals, in gleeful delight,
As bees buzz the tune, of spring's bold invite.

In the purple parade, they march side by side,
With laughter so loud, they dance with great pride.
Forget all the worries, let colors just blend,
For fun in the garden is never to end.

So gather your joy, with petals so shy,
In whispers of purple, we all learn to fly.
A symphony crafted, in nature's own voice,
Each bloom is a wink, come join the rejoice!

Beneath the Violet Skies

Under violet skies, the jokes take their flight,
The clouds throw confetti, what a silly sight!
A parade of rainbows, in mischievous glee,
The sun winks down, at the world's jubilee.

The daisies wear hats, with a sketchy design,
While tulips tell tales, that intertwine.
A breeze carries laughter, in giggles and sighs,
As the world spins around, beneath violet skies.

With every gust, comes a ticklish spell,
As the petals all giggle, like they're under a bell.
When shadows unite, for a comical chase,
Not a creature in sight, just laughter to embrace.

Though twilight approaches, the joy stays in reach,
With whimsy and wonder, the flowers each teach.
In this silly garden, where daffodils rise,
Life's a big joke, beneath violet skies.

A Woven Tale of Floral Delights

In a garden where posies dance,
Bees waltz by, in a floral trance.
Petals giggle, colors bound,
As laughter weaves through nature's sound.

Hats of flowers, they tip and bow,
Trying to impress the old, wise cow.
A daffodil slips on a dew,
Sneezing pollen—oh, how true!

Bumblebees in tiny suits,
Holding tea parties with lady fruits.
Sunflowers gossip with big, bold grins,
While dandelions meditate with spins.

So let your worries drift away,
Join the fun in this floral sway.
With every bloom, a chuckle grows,
In this garden, anything goes!

Vibrant Echoes in the Breeze

A breeze whispers secrets near the creek,
While daisies share tales that make me squeak.
With tulips boasting their fashion flair,
Even the weeds can't help but stare.

Morning glories stretch and yawn,
While geraniums blush at the dawn.
A sunflower poses, trying to flex,
As butterflies chuckle, "What the heck?"

Dandelions float like fluffy dreams,
In multi-colored pools, laughter beams.
Ladybugs wearing spots so grand,
Dare each other to stroll the land.

With every giggle and flapping wing,
The world feels lighter; oh, how it swings!
In nature's party, join the tease,
Let joy be carried upon the breeze!

Harmonies of a Violet Heart

In the garden of giggles, a violet sings,
With melodies woven from spring's bright flings.
Grasshoppers join with a tap-tap beat,
As crickets perform with nimble feet.

Roses blushing in sun's golden glow,
Sharing puns with those who grow slow.
A hellebore chiming a silly tune,
While foxgloves laugh—oh, to be a bloom!

Petunias pirouette, full of grace,
In a race with the daisies, what a chase!
With hummingbirds adding a dash of flair,
Serenading the blooms with tunes to share.

Each petal sways, alive with jest,
In violet hearts, we laugh the best.
So unleash your giggles, let them start,
Join the chorus of this floral heart!

Serenading Shadows at Sundown

As shadows dance in twilight's embrace,
Petals whisper tales, sharing space.
Evening buds stretch, yawning wide,
But sunflowers hold their heads with pride.

The moon peeks in, all silver and bright,
Chortling at flowers in the soft night.
A rose jokes, "What a funny sight,
My neighbor's scent? A true fright!"

The daisies twinkle like stars in bloom,
While violets blush, dispelling gloom.
Reclining leaves take a gentle nap,
While beetles form a nighttime rap.

So here's to the blooms and shadows that play,
Making merriment at the end of the day.
In the garden of laughter, let's not frown,
For joy blooms brightly when shadows drown!

The Scent of Sun-drenched Violets

In fields where giggles dare to dance,
The flowers wear a funny pants.
Their laughter sways with every breeze,
A joke that's tickled by the trees.

Bees buzz around, quite out of tune,
Laughing at the sun and moon.
They sip on nectar, sticky treats,
While petals giggle, making beats.

The sun shines bright, a golden wink,
As blooms tiptoe to the bathroom sink.
They wash their faces with morning dew,
And toss their petals, quite askew.

So, here's to flowers with a flair,
In violet hues, beyond compare.
Their scent a giggle, blooming fun,
In every petal, laughter's spun.

Painted Skies of Soft Regrets

The sunset paints with spills of red,
A canvas where the clouds have fled.
They trip on hues, a color clash,
While stars above prepare to dash.

Each brushstroke drips, a comical sight,
A pastel giggle, holding tight.
With every stroke, they tickle fate,
As colors blend and hesitate.

The moon looks down, a sly old chap,
In giggles wrapped, he takes a nap.
While constellations play their game,
And dance around without a shame.

Soft regrets in colors bright,
A gallery of laughter's light.
In every shade, a chuckle hides,
In painted skies, mischief bides.

Whispers of a Blooming Journey

A sprout once said, 'I'll grow up big!'
Yet stumbled on a friendly twig.
The branches chuckled, 'What a sight!'
As blossoms bloomed with pure delight.

They whispered tales of roots and dirt,
Of little seeds that wore a shirt.
Each leaf a laugh, each bud a cheer,
In gardens filled with joy and fear.

A pollen party, oh so grand,
Where daisies danced, a merry band.
The roses blushed in shades of pink,
As poppies giggled, 'What do you think?'

So off they go, to chase the sun,
A funny journey, just begun.
With whispers soft and laughter loud,
The blooms parade, so bright and proud.

Tapestry of Fading Colors

In autumn's grasp, the leaves come down,
A jolly slide across the town.
In reds and golds, they trip and fall,
Creating laughter, nature's ball.

Each leaf a joke, a playful tease,
They whirl about in gusty breeze.
The crunch beneath, a symphony,
Of shades that giggle, wild and free.

As daylight wanes, the hues grow bold,
They wrap us up in stories told.
With fading colors, spirits rise,
A tapestry of funny skies.

So cherish moments, fleeting grace,
In each swirl, a smile leaves its trace.
For in this dance of fall's embrace,
We find the joy in nature's face.

Through the Mist of Purple Haze

In a garden where giggles bloom,
Purple clouds dance like a broom.
Gnomes wear hats a tad too tall,
While butterflies trip, trying to sprawl.

The scent of mischief fills the air,
Fairy floss spins, a sugary lair.
Flowers chuckle at bees in flight,
"Buzz off!" they yell, what a silly sight!

An owl hoots jokes from the tree,
"Why did the grape stop? To let out a 'pee!'"
Laughter erupts in this leafy maze,
Through the mist of purple haze.

A cat with socks walks a tightrope,
Sipping tea whilst sharing hope.
"Why can't we all just stick together?"
Socks replied, "Let's do this forever!"

The Palette of Evening Stars

As twilight paints with a clumsy hand,
Colors spill like a bowl of sand.
Canaries wear hats, in shades so bright,
Dancing to tunes, it's a silly sight.

Fireflies can't help but blink in chat,
"What's green and sings? Elvis Parsley, that!"
Stars twinkle back, full of delight,
Chasing moonbeams in the night.

Butterflies wear evening gowns like pros,
While crickets recite Shakespeare, now who knows?
Laughter resounds as the sun takes its leave,
With a wink and a nod, we believe.

The night is a canvas of chuckles and glee,
Where jellybeans grin from the foot of a tree.
This palette of stars will forever stay,
Painting joy in their own wacky way.

Conversations in Shades of Plum

Two plums sat chatting on a swing,
Discussing hot tea and the latest fling.
"Did you hear about the peach's new hat?"
"It's made of fuzz, how silly is that?"

Lemonade wishes it could join the fun,
While grapes roll by, ready to run.
"Why don't they just relax and sit still?"
Dandelions laugh, they have all the thrill.

Under a shade, all friends unite,
Talking about socks and the moon's fright.
"Why did the tomato turn red?" they cheer,
"Because it saw the salad dressing, oh dear!"

In shades of plum, they share their brains,
Trading giggles like candy canes.
With laughter so bright, it fills the space,
These fruity conversations, a joyful race.

Reflections in a Lush Mirage

In a mirror pond, giggles collide,
Frogs wear sunglasses, full of pride.
"Ribbit me this, ribbit me that,
What's a frog's favorite game? Croquet, how about that?"

Willow trees whisper secrets so sweet,
Giggling as squirrels scamper on their feet.
A dance-off begins with a twirl and a hop,
"Who can out-joke this candy shop?"

A reflection ripples as laughter churns,
With a wink and a giggle, for joy one yearns.
Moments of glee float like a balloon,
In this lush mirage, we sing to the moon.

Ticklish breezes carry the jest,
With every chuckle, we feel so blessed.
So come take a seat, join the spree,
In this mirage, it's all about glee!

Dreamcatcher Under Purple Canopies

Beneath the leaves, a dream set free,
A squirrel danced like it was three.
With twirls and spins, it stole the show,
While flowers giggled, putting on a glow.

The owls debated who could hoot best,
As butterflies played, putting skills to the test.
A bumbling bee fell into the stew,
Buzzed out a tune, and then it just flew.

Rabbits in bow ties joined the spree,
Painting the trees with a bumblebee spree.
They laughed at mushrooms who wore silly hats,
While chasing shadows and chirping chats.

Under purple skies, everything's grand,
With giggles and chuckles in this woodland band.
Each creature a jester, full of delight,
In a dreamcatcher's web, spun a comical night.

A Symphony of Botanicals

In the garden, a band takes the stage,
With daisies strumming on a leafy page.
The roses blushed, shy in their bloom,
While violets hummed a sweet little tune.

Tall sunflowers waved like they just don't care,
While ferns did the cha-cha, twisting in the air.
The daisies giggled, tickling the grass,
As daisies and petals formed a flowered class.

A dandelion trumpet, loud and clear,
Said, "I'm the king, come lend me your ear!"
The tulips chuckled at his royal flair,
While zen-like lilies floated without a care.

Thus blooms and blades played day and night,
Creating a symphony, a rare delight.
In this botanical show, the fun won't cease,
With laughter and music, nature's masterpiece.

The Nostalgia of Emerging Blooms

A bud recalls the day of its birth,
When life unfurled, oh, what a mirth!
It sported colors, wild and bright,
As bees came buzzing with sheer delight.

The daisies swapped tales of sunny days,
Of feisty winds and sunbeam plays.
Planting memories, they sparked a jest,
With whispers of petals, they quickly confessed.

Old trees giggle at the new flower crowd,
Swaying joyfully, standing up proud.
While the pond reflected a comedy act,
As frogs leaped nearby, ready to attract.

In the garden's heart, nostalgia reigns,
As laughter blossoms, and joy remains.
With every new bloom, there's a story to tell,
In the language of flowers, life's silly spell.

Wandering Through Plum-Painted Woods

In woods of purple, I took a stroll,
Where nature's laughter played a leading role.
Bushes were jesters, trees wore a grin,
Rabbits were squirrels, let the fun begin!

Mushrooms sprang up like little balloons,
Revealing their secrets and funny tunes.
Acorns conspired with leaves in their chat,
Giggling together, imagine that!

The brook gurgled jokes like a jokester bold,
And rocks whispered tales, oh the fun they told!
As I danced through blossoms in wild jubilation,
The woods held a party, pure celebration!

With plum-painted skies and whimsical frames,
Magic and laughter danced with their names.
In these charming woods, laughter is free,
As joy paints the path, come wander with me!

Paintings of Earthy Whispers

In a canvas of grass, a cat takes a sit,
Wishing the world would come take a wit.
The flowers all giggle, oh what a tease,
As they sway in the wind, dancing with ease.

A turtle in shades, he thinks he's so sleek,
Waddles on by, thinks he's quite chic.
The daisies all snicker, their petals in bloom,
Whispering secrets, they'll fill up the room.

The squirrels are plotting a heist on the seed,
While robins are jiving, all dancing to lead.
The sun is a painter, with strokes of pure gold,
Brushes the earth with a story untold.

Oh, let's raise a toast to this whimsical play,
Where laughter and colors come out to sway.
In the paintings of whispers, we'll frolic, we'll sing,
In this funny old world, it's a joyous fling.

Colors that Sing

A purple potato wearing a hat,
Dances in the fridge, now isn't that fat?
The broccoli's laughing, it's tickled by steam,
As carrots start plotting to plot out a scheme.

The red chili pepper is feeling quite hot,
But the peas roll their eyes, say, 'you're not!'
Each color a note in this veggie review,
With cabbage on drums, keepin' rhythm so true.

The sunflower joins in with a big, sunny cheer,
Tickling the corn with its golden front tier.
Together they're jiving, the greens and the reds,
As laughter erupts, so much fun to be fed.

Oh color that sings, what a raucous delight,
A banquet of giggles that starts with a bite.
Let's relish this moment, as flavors collide,
With a laughter-filled feast, where joy cannot hide.

Garden of Delicate Hues

In a garden so bright with its delicate shades,
A gopher named Gary is digging up trades.
The roses are blushing, the violets in flair,
While daisies are gossiping without any care.

A butterfly flutters, it thinks it can sing,
But lands on a flower that says, 'What a fling!'
The petals are tickled, they giggle and sway,
While clouds look down, thinking, 'What a display!'

Crickets are crooning their nighttime delight,
As moonbeams are shimmering softly in white.
In this playful oasis, the colors collide,
With smiles quite tasty, like chocolate confide.

Oh garden of shades where the laughter's a tune,
With whispers that echo beneath the bright moon.
Let's twirl in the petals, rejoice in the cheer,
In this quirky tableau, let's spread joy and dear.

Murmurs of the Blossoming World

In a world all a-bloom, a duck's on the loose,
Waddling quite funny right next to the goose.
With whispers and chuckles, the flowers all smile,
As dandelions jiggle in a comical style.

A bumblebee buzzes, declares it's a star,
While tulips are cheering, 'We knew you'd go far!'
Amidst all the merriment, petals fall down,
In a riot of colors, no hint of a frown.

The whispers of blossoms share tales from the breeze,
As pansies recount their own sweet little tease.
A comet of hues like a laugh in the air,
Sprinkles down joy like a whimsical prayer.

Oh murmurs of blooms, your humor's supreme,
In a garden of giggles, life flows like a dream.
With petals and laughter, the world finds its way,
In this blossoming chorus, we dance, spin, and play.

Veils of Fragrant Air

A whiff of spring bursts forth,
As noses twitch in delight,
Bees buzzing with mirthful cheer,
Chasing scents till nightfall's light.

Sneaky petals dance and sway,
In breezes teasing the stroll,
Giggling leaves whisper aloud,
Tickling pollen, a playful role.

Wandering through color fields,
Where aromas play hide and seek,
Oh, what chaos these blooms weave,
Mischief found in every cheek!

Silly thoughts among the blooms,
What if flowers wore a hat?
Would they tip and wink at us,
In a floral soirée so phat?

Traces of Soft Bloom

With every step, surprise awaits,
Petals splatter on the ground,
Nature's jokes, oh how they prank,
Making footsteps softly bound.

The garden holds its giggles close,
Each stem a stand-up comic,
Dandelions puff puff pass,
A joke so wildly ironic.

Silly bees in tiny suits,
Dance in circles, prancing free,
While butterflies in silly hats,
Crash the party, can't you see?

A tumble here, a stumble there,
The earth laughs with us, oh so bright,
Creating joy in every nook,
Who knew blooms could be this light?

Hues of Enchanted Evenings

As twilight wraps the garden tight,
Colors mingle in a swirl,
Whispers of the day's delight,
Where giggles of the flowers twirl.

Fireflies play hide and seek,
With shades of purple, pink, and blue,
Caught in laughter, what a peek,
A floral masquerade's debut!

In this enchanted, silly spree,
The moon peeks in, ready to glow,
Twirling blossoms spill their secrets,
In a show that steals the show!

Tickled petals hum a tune,
As night unfolds its sweet display,
Who would guess that blooms can grin,
In a most enchanting, funny way?

The Language of Floral Secrets

In the garden's hidden chat,
Petals gossip, talk and play,
Stems lean in with a little laugh,
Sharing secrets of the day.

A rose winks, a daisy giggles,
In hues of joy they weave their jest,
Telling tales of breeze and chirps,
With nature's humor manifest.

The tulips blush with rosy tales,
As violets whisper sweet confessions,
Like a floral play on a stage,
Bursting forth in silly expressions.

Oh, what a language blooms retell,
With soft petals, laughter, and cheer,
Who could resist their playful words,
In a world where humor's dear?

Mysteries of the Indigo Evening

In twilight's hue, the cats conspire,
To steal the moon from the sky's high wire.
A giggling breeze, a dance of delight,
As fireflies blink through the soft, gentle night.

Old dogs chase shadows, with grace so divine,
While pigeons debate on a porch's fine line.
A riddle of laughter hangs in the air,
While squirrels are plotting who gets the last pear.

Whispers of stars tease the curtains of dusk,
Every heartbeat giggles with a playful husk.
Beneath the vast sky, as mysteries churn,
A raucous delight makes the candles burn.

So gather your friends, for the evening is bright,
With jokes and odd antics under pale moonlight.
Let's dance with the shadows and sing with the breeze,
In this evening of laughter, we do what we please.

Faded Stories Beneath the Boughs

Under the branches, tales intertwine,
Of gnomes who steal socks, and that garden of twine.
A breeze whips through, carrying the jest,
As crickets chirp secrets, they never digress.

The trees chuckle softly, their bark full of cheer,
While raccoons plot mischief, with nary a fear.
An owl with a monocle watches the show,
Giving winks and nods to the squirrels below.

With acorns for tickets, let the madcap play,
Where laughter grows louder as night takes the day.
Beneath boughs of wonder, we all are so bold,
With stories of giggles that never grow old.

So pull up a chair, under starlit embrace,
And share a few laughs in this magical space.
For life has its wonders, both silly and grand,
In the shade of the tree, let joy take a stand.

Embracing the Fragrance of Twilight

As dusk settles gently, it brings forth a jest,
With shadows that dance, which we love the best.
The cat on the fence gives a theatrical yawn,
While the dog sings a tune till the early dawn.

Fireflies are flashers, in sequined delight,
Reminding the stars they can show off tonight.
A whiff of mischief drifts right on the breeze,
With crickets composing quirky melodies.

The roses get jealous, their petals all puffed,
While daisies argue, their heads a bit stuffed.
The moon rolls its eyes at the antics below,
As giggles and snickers just seem to grow.

So let's raise a toast to the evening's odd lore,
With laughter and joy that we simply adore.
In twilight's sweet hug, as the day bids goodbye,
We embrace every moment, just you and I.

Shadows in a Field of Color

In a field where the colors like candy all bloom,
Dance shadows like jesters, with laughter and zoom.
The daisies are plotting an outrageous spree,
While a butterfly teases, 'Come dance along with me!'

Sunflowers sway with a whimsical air,
Challenging rabbits to hop without care.
While bees giggle softly, their buzz a sweet song,
In this vibrant carnival where all feel they belong.

A picnic unfolds, with pies flying high,
As ants play tag on a hot buttered pie.
With grapes launching splashy, a fruity delight,
The joy of the moment makes everything bright.

So let's skip through the colors, from red to the blue,
Where shadows are playful, and the laughter is true.
In this field of delight, come join in the fun,
For every bright sunset brings a joke just begun.

The Art of Wildflower Breath

In a meadow dance the blooms,
With noses twitching, no more glooms.
They laugh at bees, they tease the sun,
In nature's whiff, they've lots of fun.

With pollen jokes and ticklish grass,
These flowers party, oh, what a gas!
They swirl and twirl, they sip the rain,
Creating scents that entertain.

A daisy winks at a shy bluebell,
'Hey there, buddy, let's cast a spell!'
They've formed a club, they're in their prime,
Collecting laughter, one petal at a time.

So when you stroll through nature's show,
Listen closely, hear the flow.
For wildflowers giggle - it's quite the treat,
In their fragrant world, life can't be beat!

Petals on a Gentle Breeze

Petals drift down from heights unseen,
Whirling like dancers in a bright scene.
They tumble and bounce with carefree style,
Inviting a laugh, evoking a smile.

The wind plays tricks, tossing them wide,
A cheerful game, a fun-filled ride.
They flap like flags with a joyful cheer,
Creating a show that's oh-so-clear.

A violet shouts, 'Hey, catch my spin!'
Follow me, friend, where should we begin?
With every gust, they leap and play,
A flower's frolic, on display.

So next time you see petals fly,
Remember their giggles, don't be shy.
Join the fun, let your heart agree,
In nature's laugh, find pure glee!

Murmurs of the Flowering Hour

As twilight whispers, blooms arise,
Their giggles mixing with soft sighs.
In the flower bed, a chatty crowd,
Unfolding tales, lively and loud.

They gossip 'bout the bees that buzz,
And how the snails can cause a fuzz.
'Oh look! Here comes the bumblebee!'
He's clumsier than a kid when he's free.

In pots and patches, laughter swells,
With every tale, the garden tells.
A dandelion jokes, 'I've got no green!'
Chasing the dreams of being seen.

So join the chatter, lend an ear,
To flowery whispers, bright and clear.
In this blooming hour, let joy empower,
Nature's humor, the flowering power!

Colors Dripping from Dusk

As the sun dips, paints the sky,
Colors drip down, oh my, oh my!
The flowers giggle, 'We can't go to sleep,
Dusk looks like candy, into us it will creep.'

Orange and purple, they swirl with grace,
A palette splashed on nature's face.
They beckon the stars to come join the mix,
With splatters of laughter, they dance with tricks.

A tulip sings, 'Let's paint the night!'
While daisies cheer, 'Oh isn't it bright?'
They blend and mingle, 'What next can we do?'
In colors so vivid, a rainbow anew.

So take a moment, watch the show,
As dusk drips colors, fun to bestow.
In nature's canvas, let joy take flight,
For laughter and color make everything right!

Veils of Floral Sighs

In the garden, blooming bright,
Bumblebees in silly flight.
Petals dance in breezy play,
Who knew flowers knew ballet?

Hats made of petals, so bizarre,
Worn by daisies, oh so far!
Sunflowers giggle, swaying high,
So unlike the shy blue sky.

A rose told jokes, quite absurd,
But spoke so softly, barely heard.
Tulips chuckled, sprightly and spry,
Wondering when they'd learn to fly!

In this patch of sheer delight,
Nature's laughter feels so right.
Though bees may buzz about and tease,
We're all just flowers, swaying with ease.

Threads of Indigo Memories

Indigo threads in the twilight,
Stitched together with pure delight.
Threads of laughter, a weaving spree,
Making memories, oh so free!

In a quilt of giggles, stitched well,
Each patch tells a funny tale to tell.
Did the daisies prank the tulips too?
When petals fall, who knew what they'd do?

A violet wore shades, feeling cool,
Strutting about, the garden's own fool.
While marigolds mocked the morning sun,
Claiming their shine was just too fun!

So gather 'round those vibrant hues,
Share a chuckle while sipping brews.
Together we'll weave the finest thread,
Of laughter and joy in the garden spread.

Soft Murmurs in Lavender Fields

In lavender fields, whispers fly,
Flowers giggling as bees hover by.
Each breeze carries a tickling chime,
Nature's jokes, perfectly in rhyme!

The lavender called, "Join in the fun!"
While roses blushed under setting sun.
Dandelions danced, tossed by the wind,
Swaying and spinning, oh where to begin?

Butterflies flutter with a cheeky grin,
A moth tripped over, where to begin?
"Not in my garden!" the lilacs exclaimed,
As daisies giggled, completely unclaimed!

Fields of laughter, a sight to behold,
Stories of blooms, a treasure untold.
We linger and laugh till the daylight ends,
In this floral realm where joy transcends.

Pastel Secrets Beneath the Blossoms

Pastel secrets on petals shine,
Whispers of mischief, oh divine!
Flower friends giggling, oh what a sight,
Plotting their pranks from morning to night!

The daisies dared the roses to sing,
While peonies blushed, feeling like spring.
They laughed at the tulips in disarray,
Who tripped on their roots like kids at play!

With every bloom, a laugh unfolds,
Petal confessions and stories told.
Beside the blooms, in playful trust,
Where bringing joy is a must!

So join this garden of pastel dreams,
Where laughter flows like gentle streams.
And under the blossoms, secrets will grow,
As petals sway to the humor's flow!

Serenade Under Violet Skies

Under skies so purple and grand,
We dance with jokes, as clowns we stand.
The flowers giggle, petals sway,
Oh, what a sight on this violet day!

A bee tried to join our little fun,
Buzzing around, he thinks he's won.
But oh dear bee, you've got no style,
You're dancing like a fool, all the while!

Frogs croak laughter, their leaps so bold,
While squirrels share secrets, stories untold.
We twirl and spin, the moonlight joins,
In a symphony of giggles, the heart rejoins.

As the twilight blankets, we bid adieu,
To all the laughter that we brewed anew.
Under violet skies, we'll meet next time,
With more silly pranks, and rhythm in rhyme!

Memories in Blossom Time

In the garden, blooms start to show,
Memories of laughter begin to flow.
We planted joy in rows so bright,
And watch it grow from morning's light.

The gnomes stand guard with silly grins,
As squirrels play chess and wager wins.
Each laugh a petal, floating away,
Carrying the magic of a sunny day.

Old stories told by grandpa's vine,
Like who spilled juice on the laundry line.
Each blossom a laugh, a chuckle shared,
In blossom time, love has always fared.

So let's raise a toast with lemonade,
To memories in bloom that never fade.
With each sip, a giggle we find,
In the joy of youth, forever entwined!

Scented Memories of Youth

A whiff of spring, a dash of cheer,
Rides the breeze, oh so near.
We laugh at the stains on the carpet bright,
And dance like fools under morning light.

Grass stains whisper tales of fun,
Of epic games that were never won.
Memories rich, like chocolate pie,
Oh, the tales that make us sigh!

The garden's wild, our laughter loud,
With parents watching, feeling proud.
We treasure the scents of joy we grew,
In scented days of our carefree crew.

A bouquet of giggles tucked in a vase,
Forever remembering every face.
Youth blossoms in fragrant delight,
Even as we chase the setting light!

Threads of Amethyst Wonder

Stitching dreams with threads of glee,
Amethyst wonders, just you and me.
Tickling the flowers, they bloom and sway,
As we unravel the droll today.

The bumblebee wears a tiny crown,
While tulips giggle in golden gown.
We skip through gardens, a comical sight,
Finding joy in the fluttering light.

Giggles weave in the air around,
As we leap from flower to flower, bound.
Oh, what a tapestry we create,
With every chuckle, our hearts elate.

In threads of wonder, we always play,
Clutching our laughter at the start of day.
So here's to the fun, in every hue,
With each thread woven, my friend, it's you!

A Story Written in Floral Scripts

Once upon a time in a meadow bright,
Flowers gathered for a quirky night.
A daisy told jokes, not too profound,
While the roses giggled, petals round.

A tulip tripped over a nearby weed,
Laughed out loud, 'Guess I've lost my speed!'
The marigold snickered, oh what a sight,
As they danced under the moon, pure delight.

In the breeze, their secrets did float,
Tales of mischief on a floral boat.
With every petal, a tale to spin,
The night grew warmer, laughter, their win.

So here's to blooms with humor so fine,
In scripts of laughter, they brightly shine!
Each flower a character, all unique,
Their stories written in laughter they speak.

Hues of Nightfall Whispers

In the twilight's blend of purple hues,
Petals exchanged the silliest news.
A violet blushed, dared to chime in,
'This gossip is juicy—where do I begin?'

A nightshade yawned, stretched high to display,
'What's the buzz? Don't leave me to sway!'
The pansies chuckled, clever and neat,
Made puns that echoed, impossible to beat.

With laughter that danced on the breeze so light,
They wove a tapestry of humor that night.
Whispers of petals, so perfectly spun,
In shades of the evening, they laughed like the sun.

So if you wander where blooms have a chat,
You might find a joke in a warm floral hat.
They giggle and gossip, the kings of the scene,
In hues of the night, they're vibrant and keen.

The Secret of Purple Crescendos

In a garden where mayhem tends to grow,
Petals confide in a secretive flow.
A hyacinth sang a tune with a twist,
While the orchids chuckled, not one disagreed.

'What's the secret?' a lily did pry,
'Is it laughter that makes petals fly high?'
The secrets of purple, they danced with delight,
In flower-studded chaos, they conquered the night.

A secret revealed in giggles galore,
As tulips tumbled, they begged for more.
The crescent moon winked at their silly spree,
While bees buzzed along to the floral jubilee.

So if you catch whispers of purple ascend,
Know laughter is flower's most joyous friend.
With petals in rhythm, they bloom and they sway,
In garden of laughter, they flit and they play.

Ghosts of Botanical Legends

In the dead of night when shadows creep,
Floral ghosts waltz, their secrets to keep.
Daisies whisper tales of old,
About a petunia who was bold.

With surface giggles, they rise from the bed,
Booing and cooing with laughter instead.
'Long ago,' said the sage sunflower,
'A plot thickened under the moon's power.'

Scarecrows chuckled, swaying in time,
As roses recited their legendary rhyme.
Each blossom a specter, dancing with grace,
Painting the night with a petal embrace.

So fear not the blooms that rustle and sway,
For ghosts in the garden just come out to play.
With laughter they sing, legends reborn,
In the shadows of blooms where magic is worn.

www.ingramcontent.com/pod-product-compliance
Lightning Source LLC
Chambersburg PA
CBHW071842160426
43209CB00003B/387